Narangi Days

The Untold Nostalgia of Life

BEEJA
HOUSE

ISBN: 978-81-19682-30-0

Published by: Beeja House

Printed By: Repro India Pvt. Ltd.

First Printing Edition 2024

Author Email: nair.kumarmanoj@gmail.com

Contents

Foreword

We all have read the classic Malgudi Days by the renowned author Shri R K Narayan, and later… The Sunny Days, the much-acclaimed biography of the greatest Indian opening batsman, Mr. Sunil Gavaskar, who mastered the art of facing fearsome fast bowlers, both on and off the cricket field. Both writers had their unique storytelling moments where they captured the story through the lens of the main protagonist, and it made us laugh, and cry, gave us the chills, and thrills, and brought about a few emotions within us too.

The book "The Narangi Days" is a beautiful, poignant story of Babu from the panoramic landscape of Narangi, a small army town located 25 km away from the bustling city of Guwahati in Assam. The real-life story from 1976 to 1983 captures the growing up years of Babu, his friends, his school time, playtime, his time with parents, sisters, and many more entwined into this lovely short book. Happy Reading…

The story is purely fictional, and an amalgamation and vast interpretation from author's real life experiences. Any resemblance and association with a living character/s is purely coincidental. The author is not interested to relate to any character, and has only written this book for the readers, and for their pleasure of reading.

Acknowledgements

To get your first book published is a great feeling itself, and it gives me an opportunity to thank all the people, who were involved in the journey to make this dream a reality. The dream of becoming an author of a book, written by yourself, and to be read by millions, this satisfaction is unmeasurable, and something only an author can relish in all his lifetime.

First things first, spending close to three decades in corporate marketing & sales, with office and home to focus on, a 9-7 work schedule that runs 5 days a week is a big, enormous task. This involves a lot of sacrifice, both within you, and by your family. Hence, big thanks to my wife Jayasree, and both my sons Sharath & Shyam for bearing with me in the last one year, when I was busy in the process of finalizing a core idea to write a book. All the love from sisters and blessings of my parents was instrumental for completing my journey as an author. Thanks for standing for me and with me all this while, as your patience have borne fruit, with my manuscript having reached publishing stage.

Though I always loved to motivate my sales & marketing team, it was a different experience to get inspired myself in the area of authoring a book.

The 100% credit of which will go to **Ms. Geetika Saigal**, whose first YouTube session was attended by me in early 2022, and which fuelled me to enrol to her masterclass program of three-months duration. Geetika had assured us to take us through from an ideation stage to the final publishing stage of a book, traversing through various genre. Later, I became a core member of her author's group family, and we started having sessions every Saturday and Sunday with authors, soon-to-be authors, and for people like me who had taken the first baby step in the journey to become an author.

The interactions, chatter-batter, and the insights we used to gather from these weekend programs with Geetika was blessing in disguise, as it removed the fear within us that writing is a task. She made us believe that anyone can become an author provided he/she understands, and follow the laid-down process very clearly, and meticulously to fine tune all aspects of writing a good book, whether a fiction, non-fiction, autobiography, memoirs, poetry etc. The genre selection being a key, the key elements to make your story interesting, and engaging to the readers are some of the tips gathered through the mentoring sessions with Geetika Saigal, which I always relished. Geetika has the quality knack to keep everyone in the room, whether online/offline glued to her, and will try her best to provide quality time and attention to each one in the program.

My heartfelt thanks to all the school, and college classmates; colleagues and my mentors in the journey, to keep in close touch with me on Whatsapp group, and making the sincere attempts to meet even after three decades of separation is something I cherish, and worth a mention here. Friends, am sure you will be proud of me, and will make a prompt decision to purchase the book online to read it and share your feedback here to write more often.

Last but not the least, the acknowledgement will not be complete without mentioning Geetika's support team, and Beeja house, which include Project Head Ms. Saakshi Kaushal, and the back end team, who were responsible for continuous follow-up right from the onset of masterclass sessions with Geetika, to the writing journey, till the submission of the book manuscript. Kudos to Saakshi in particular, and the Beeja Team who has been of constant help to me in this remarkable journey, and I will be forever thankful to each one of them.

Introduction

The story unfolds on a misty November morning in the year 1976, the very same year Zanjeer was released, and Bollywood got the angry young man Amitabh Bachchan and here was Babu striding forward happily towards his school located close to the mountains in Narangi, an army base located in Guwahati town of Assam state, singing a film tune.

Little did he know that a big male elephant had just entered the huge school ground, and a large group of students, staff, and onlookers had now gathered to shoo the animal back to the hills. Babu's KV school was located just 1 km below the hills, and it provided a panoramic view of the school campus.

Babu and his school friends not only had animals like elephant, deer, horses, and monkeys for constant company, but even birds mainly the eagles used to visit the school grounds in dozens, circling around to pick up a morsel of food from any of the student's tiffin.

So, when it was lunch time, Babu and his friends would rush towards the school ground, sit in a circle, and then open their tiffin boxes. The tiffins mainly had bread, chappati, and subzi. The fun moment for the kids was to throw a piece of bread or chappati on the ground, and watch how from nowhere deep in the sky, the eagle would come, pick up the piece, and again soar back into the sky. Many times, if the kids were not having good possession of their tiffin, the same eagle used to pick up the entire tiffin box and fly high upwards, making the concerned kid a laughing stock among his/her peers. Lunch break was the best time for Babu in the school, and he, Shaji and all his friends used to wait for the school bell to ring, so that the kids could rush to the main school ground for lunch and play.

So, this is Babu, the main protagonist of this story, along with his class friend and home friend Shaji, and the many characters who come into this beautiful story. This is an interesting book of 10 chapters, and each chapter smells like a fresh bean of coffee telling a unique story by itself as you read it.

Happy Reading once again…

Chapter 1

Learning Guitar

Babu's father was a strict man with Army discipline and always wanted to inculcate good habits, and new hobbies in his kids. Babu being the eldest son, his father wanted him to learn guitar at a young age. Maybe he had thought of Babu as a rockstar growing up, especially with the disco and pop culture already hitting India with Bappi Lahiri's music, and Mithun Da as Disco king of India.

He knew a man from Mangalore, who was in a barracks store, and played good guitar, hence Babu was to learn western guitar from him only.

The first day of guitar classes on a Sunday afternoon is still livid in Babu's memory. He had a class every Sunday from 4pm to 5pm. That Sunday, he reached 10 minutes early and pressed the bell of Mr Uthangi's house, but there was no response, so he knocked on the door, and the door flung open. Maybe Uthangi had expected Babu to reach at 4pm and was on his afternoon siesta.

When Babu entered the house, the drawing room was clean and tidy as he sat on the sofa. There was a cool wind blowing, maybe since it was monsoon, there was a probability of rain expected later. Due to the strong wind, the bedroom curtain flung wide, and he could see Mr & Mrs Uthangi in a tight embrace on the bed of the adjoining room. They had bare minimum clothes around them, and a bedsheet was the only cover for their modesty. In his curiosity, he could see their faces and their legs stretching out of the bedsheet in that embrace. While Mr. Uthangi was a well-built Army man, Mrs. Uthangi was a pretty slim lady with great looks and someone who made great kheer. He then recollected the first meeting when he had come last Sunday along with his Dad for an introduction to guitar class, and she had offered Kheer to them. Babu felt a schoolboy crush on the very first visit.

He continued to wait on the sofa and, just then Mr Uthangi's son came running home calling "Papa… Mama". Suddenly, both the Uthangis woke up from their sleep slumber, and seeing Babu sitting on the sofa, rushed to wrap themselves with the only bedsheet around the bed. Mr. Uthangi had only a short, while Mrs. Uthangi was only in her petticoat and blouse. While Mrs. Uthangi rushed to the bathroom, Mr. Uthangi picked a t-shirt and came straight to the drawing room to meet Babu.

Babu thought he would ask what time you came, and did you see anything, but nothing of that sort happened. Mr. Uthangi was straight onto his guitar and started playing a few beats.

He said, "Babu do you know this song?" He started playing, *'My heart is beating.. keeps on repeating, am waiting for you,'* and just went on. Babu was lost in the music and song for a moment. Being a movie freak, Babu had fond memories of this song from the movie Julie, which he had seen a month ago along with his parents & sisters.

Mr. Uthangi continued, "Babu, there are three major chords in a guitar you must know. First is D chord, then A chord, and last is C chord and, all the beats emerge from these chords only." Babu could see that Mr Uthangi's fingers was creating magic on the guitar. While the left hand fingers were pressing on the metal strings hard, the right hand had the key, which was subtly playing the strings. Babu then understood it was all a game of fingers that resulted in beautiful music emerging from the guitar.

Then suddenly Mr Uthangi stopped playing guitar and said, "Babu, now you try and play the same song using the three chords on the guitar." That was the first time Babu played the guitar, but when he pressed his tiny, boyish finger on the metal string, he felt a slight pain, but the beats were not being heard. Mr.Uthangi got up from his seat and pressed Babu's fingers a little hard on the metal string that's when magic happened and musical beats started filling the room. At that moment, Mrs. Uthangi entered the room, dressed in a pink saree, with water dripping from her hair. She had lemon juice and two pieces of cake on a plate and came to offer us both. She kept it on the table, pressed my cheeks, and said, "Babu, you are playing well." That was a kind of inspiration for a novice like Babu, who was in his first guitar class. The spark of appreciation from his first crush made Babu press the metal strings much harder, play the keys with his right hand, and the music started flowing as sweet as ever.

The classes continued and Babu discovered many more musical gems on guitar like 'Ajeeb Dastaan Hai', 'Khoya Khoya Chaand', and so on.

So, this was his first meeting with Uthangi. We will hear another interesting part of his meeting with Uthangi at a sports meet in a later chapter.

Chapter 2

Babu's singing debut@ school

First day of class-II in KV school, Narangi, this scene is quite vivid in the memories of Babu even today. That first impact was so powerful that when someone in the family asks today, Babu was always ready to belt out a song, to an extent that his best friend and classmate, Shaji always used to envy him for his singing calibre. Little did Shaji know that it was their bestie in class Molly belting out *'Ek Din Bik Jayega..Mati ke Mol'* that inspired Babu to sing an Amitabh song in the class that day. It was *'Yeh Dosti Hum Nahi Todenge'* from the movie Sholay. Babu had seen the movie Sholay maybe a dozen times in the Rhino Hall located in Narangi.

That first day of school still reverberates with Babu. The teacher came to the class, took attendance, and asked each student his or her name, and their respective hobbies. He still recalls when the teacher asked Molly his name, he uttered Molly Barnendra Kumar Rao.. in short MBK Rao. Molly was from Andhra state, a dusky guy, who was brilliant in academics, and a good speaker too. When the teacher asked Molly about his hobbies, he told her how he liked reading, and singing, to which the teacher asked him to sing a song. There it was, Molly belting out the song 'Ek din bik jayega..maati ke mol..' and he went on and on, singing the complete song. Babu and the entire class was in awe of him, and clapped a lot after his song. When it was Babu's turn, and the teacher asked him, Babu also listed singing and playing cricket, football. Then the teacher asked Babu to sing a song. Since Sholay was fresh on his mind, and having considered Shaji as his Veeru, he blurted out the song.. 'Yeh dosti hum nahi todenge..' looking at Shaji from the corner of his eye. The class loved the song, and clapped for Babu. At that moment Babu realized that singing is in his blood, with both his parents being good singers in family functions, when they visited their native place in Kerala.

Since it's the singing genre of this story, another vivid memory of childhood that Babu had was during one of his summer holidays. He had visited a relative's house on a Sunday along with his parents, and sisters. After the singing session of elders was over, and after a sumptuous lunch, it was the turn of the kids to hone their talent. Lissy aunty whose place Babu had visited asked them to sing a song, he and his two sisters looked at each other, and immediately blurted out the song "Jahan chaar yaar mil jaye wahin raat ho Gulza…r" the iconic song from the movie Sharaabi, which was such a hit those days. Babu had bought an audio cassette of the movie, which could play out the dialogues scene by scene, along with all the songs of the movie. Poor Lissy Aunty did not know the Hindi song that Babu and his sisters had *rattofied* (memorized the song completely) and sang it in full gusto much to the delight of all the friends and relatives present there.

Chapter 3

Lunch time Masti

If lunch time was all about eagles hovering around you in the large playground of the school, trying to catch the student's tiffin or food, then there was another area, which Babu and his friends were very fond of. That was a lunch canteen operated by Varghese uncle, a man with a big moustache as long as Veerappan, and sitting mostly in a Dhoti and shirt but, the sight and smell of crispy dosa he used to prepare, makes every kid in the class like Babu to just stand and witness the art of making crispy, tasty dosa. It may sound ridiculous that this crispy plain dosa was available for Rs.1/- while the tastier masala dosa was for your taking at Rs.2/- and this was during the period of 1978 to 1983, when Babu spent most of his school days in Narangi.

Varghese uncle will sit around the large black tawa, heated to the maximum under a flame. Then at the press of a button at 12.30pm of lunch time, he will throw little water on the tawa and swishhhhhhhhhhhhhhh there is a sound from the tawa and then Varghese uncle will throw the dosa batter on the tawa, and use a round spoon used to make the dosa round shaped. When it goes crispy, he turns it around, then if someone wants masala, it will be placed then, and the dosa goes another turn. It's ready to be taken, and is served to you on a plate for Rs.2/- and if this feeling was not bliss, what else could it be friends.

Babu was lucky he could experience this in his school days, and eat it too for a continuous period of 5 years, every lunch time. Those days 2 or 5 paise was the pocket money given to every child going to school. It was that precious. If today's kid were told about it, they would laugh aloud and tell..."Babu, are you joking my dear?" But, these are facets of a life, well lived and enjoyed by Babu during the glorious period of 1978 to 1983.

You will know more of Varghese uncle, and his versatility, when you read the chapter on Bishwakarma Puja celebrations in Narangi. So hold on to this book friends.

Chapter 4

Bond of Friendship and Games Galore

In the school, Babu's best friends were Shaji, Molly, Arindam, and Harish. Then, there was a friendship gang after school, ready and waiting for Babu at home, which included Bishnu, Biju, and Shaji of course. Shaji was the common factor among both his school and home friends. If school was all about participating in school periods, recess time enjoyment, and games period, then post school time at home was games galore starting at 4pm, and going till 6pm everyday.

Games used to be cricket invariably, and the best part being it was unisex, as both boys and girls used to combine form two teams, and play the game of cricket. Babu's sisters, Shaji's sisters, Bishnu's sister, and Biju's sister also used to join the game of cricket. The two team captains used to be Shaji and Babu himself, and they would pick their team. If Bishnu is part of Babu's team, then Biju will form part of Shaji's team. On very rare occasions, Babu & Shaji form part of the same team, while Bishnu & Biju will be the opponents. But on such occasions, they used to belt the opponents, hence decided to be on the opposite side, and pick the team accordingly. The team used to be well balanced, and one used to get an exciting game each day. On Sundays, there used to be a mega game, wherein Babu's parents used to watch it from their balcony, and even give commentary to enthuse the children playing the game.

Both Babu & Shaji were fast bowlers, and always opened the attack for their respective team. It was tennis ball first, and then they graduated to rubber deuce ball, and finally to cork ball by the time they reached class 9. Playtime used to be 4pm to 6pm everyday, and once Babu's father arrived home, Babu and his sisters would reach home, freshen up, and complete homework, and show it to Mom & Dad.

One interesting incident, which still reverberates through the minds of Babu all the time, was on a Sunday evening, when the family had booked movie tickets for Hindi movie "Hum Kisise Kum Nahin". Babu was playing football with his friends. It was 5pm, and his mother was calling. Babu was now supposed to come home, take bath, wear a new dress, and get ready for the movie show, since his father would come around 5.45pm, and then they would go for the movie on the Lambretta scooter.

After 5 minutes, there was a loud cry from the playground, and Shaji ran to Babu's house, and informed his mother that Babu has cut his leg, and is bleeding profusely. His mom informed someone to go to Babu's father's office, and inform him to come soon. What happened thereafter Babu does not remember, and only his father narrated the post incident to him. He was taken to a military surgeon, who seemed to have put him on sedation, and applied 5 to 6 stitches on the wound, which was quite apparent, whenever Babu looked at his left hand. Thus, whenever Babu is reminded of the movie "Hum Kisise Kum Nahin", this incident comes straight to his mind. His mother even makes fun of him now that if only he had listened to her, and come home on time, that incident could have been averted.

Cricket and football were not the only games, which Babu, his sisters, and all their friends in Narangi played. The games used to change as per the season of spring, summer, autumn (rains) and winter. There was badminton, cycling, gallery, kho-kho, kabaddi, pithu.. you name the game, and Babu and his friends would have played it in Narangi. The competitive spirit in each of these games was to be seen to be believed. Such was the intensity, and involvement that on Sundays, the parents of all kids would be watching the matches live as if an international tournament was going on. There were proper scorecards written on notebooks, with batsman & bowler as per each team's line-up. It was fun throughout each game.

When arranging the school notebooks for classwork and homework, then Babu would give the full credit to his mother, who would meticulously put brown paper on each notebook, and put the corresponding label marked C/W or H/W affixed on each of the school notebooks. This made Babu and his sisters to only focus on their studies, and get good marks for their exams. Babu used to be in the 3rd position in the class, and it was always a toss-up between Molly and Arindam for the 1st and second positions. However, in class 7, the tables turned, and for the first time Babu became first in the class, followed by Molly and Arindam. That was a moment to cherish for Babu, and to this day he still remembers his father gifted him a HMT watch to wear having secured 1st rank in the school. But that was the only time he secured first position in school. His sister however was brilliant and would top the class every year.

What is school time without some crushes? Babu also had his share of crushes. It started with Mrs.

Uthangi, who served him kheer during his guitar classes for 3 months. Then came a beautiful girl named Divya Bakshi, who joined school in class 6. She was pretty, fair, and came from UP. She spoke very well, and Babu used to look at her many times, admiring her beauty and grace.

Another KV school fun outing was being taken to a movie theatre, wherein the entire class would be shown a movie to enjoy with snacks and soft drinks. It used to be one full day of fun. Babu had the opportunity to watch movies like Gandhi, the Oscar-winning movie of Richard Attenborough, Asrani's comedy movie Hum Nahin Sudhrenge, 3D movie My Dear Kuttichathan, and a few other nature's wildlife exploration movies. It was fun watching it with school friends, and it gives goosebumps to Babu when someone reminds him of those days.

KV schools made kids an all-rounder in life, and that's something Babu will thank his school, teachers, and parents for having nurtured that ambition within him to excel not only in academics but also in sports and extra-curricular activities. These extra-curricular activities include participation in debates, extempore, dumb charades, essays, quizzes, and even calligraphy contests. His mother and father were the inspiration behind the success of Babu and his sisters in academics, sports, and extra-curricular activities.

Even to this day, his mother has retained those certificates or marksheets of Babu & his sisters from Class 5 to Class 10, and sometimes going through the certificate collection, does bring a few drops of tears in the eyes of Babu.

Chapter 5

Maggi Test

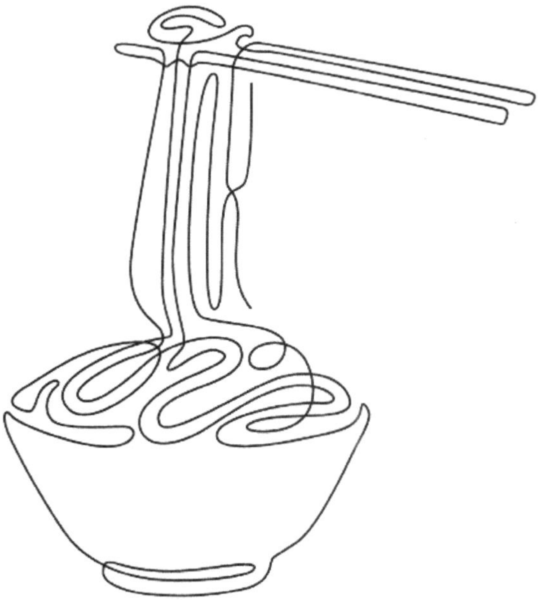

Another interesting story that Babu wants to share was the Maggi distribution in the school sometime in 1982. That entire day is still vivid in the memories of Babu. The day started with the morning prayers in the school. After the prayer, all students were made to stand in a line. The principal announced that a special food packet (2 each) would be given to each student to carry home, and show it to their parents, who would cook it for them, after adding vegetables to it, boil, and serve it hot in the evening.

All the kids were excited about getting the yellow coloured packets with "Maggi" written on the centre of the pack. After the assembly was over, and all the children reached their respective classes, the excitement only got further increased among the kids. Babu could see Divya holding the Maggi packets close to her heart, and hugging it as if it was a Barbie doll. Few girls kept it in their bag immediately, while some were flaunting it by keeping it on their desks.

Babu could see the boys were more creative, and their curiosity had no limits. Some were playing catch-catch with the packets on the back bench, and the packets were hurled up in the air for other kids to catch it. The one who drops will be made docket and asked to carry all the Maggi packets on his head from the door to his seat. There were a few extra smart boys in the class, who could not hold their curiosity till evening and decided to open the packet to see what was inside. They all saw a white, coiled hard stuff inside, and when someone pressed it, it broke by the impact. The curiosity only increased among the boys. One boy was a karate champ of the class, who decided to break the stuff into multiple pieces and give it to each boy in the class. The boy was Biju, who was a good friend of Babu, and thus Babu also got a piece. Now the million-dollar question was who would eat it first. All this while, the girls were also anxiously looking at Biju and the boys sitting on the back bench. Suddenly, Biju came to the centre of the class where the teacher stood to take the class, put the piece into his mouth, and started biting and chewing it. Seeing Biju eating Maggi made temptations go wild among other kids, and Babu also relished the taste of this new item. Maggi tasted bland, but it had a salty snack taste to it. It was then decided all kids would share, and eat one packet in the class, and one would be taken home for the parents. The packet also had a small packet inside, but most of the kids thought it to be a waster, and discarded the same. The afternoon walk back from school to home had a rare sight of many kids eating raw Maggi, so much so that the subway had lots of yellow Maggi wrappers for the road housekeeping staff to clean the next day.

Only later in the evening, when they all reached home and gave the packet to their parents, they were told it was the masala sweetener, which was to be added to the solid piece of Maggi, and boiled in water for 5 minutes, mixed, stir, and only then have it. Some of the parents cut vegetables to boil along with Maggi and give it to the kids. Hence, that Narangi night in the lives of all the kids including Babu was Maggi night, and the next day they walked to the school, each one narrating their stories of Maggi eating. Truly a novel way of eating a new snack launched first time in Babu's school in the sleepy yet energetic town of Narangi.

Chapter 6
Sunday Lambretta Drive

Babu always loved riding the iconic, vintage Lambretta scooter of his father every Sunday, and Sundays used to be the family time for Babu and his sisters. The vintage Lambretta drive used to start at 5.30pm from their home after the Sunday round of games, which ended by 4.30pm. Then Babu and his sisters used to take a bath, and wear new clothes to watch Sunday movies at Rhino Hall. The single 70mm screen was the only theatre in the vicinity of their homes, and was managed by the Defence staff.

The drive in Lambretta scooter was also a unique experience, the memories of which lived with Babu even today, and he still narrates the experience to his friends. The Lambretta was a blue colour vintage classic, which was a 5-seater, and just perfect for Babu & his two sisters to go on a family drive to Rhino Hall each Sunday. Dad used to drive this mean machine, with Mom behind, and Madhu, elder of the sisters sandwiched between his parents. The fight or I could say the prized seat was at the back, and was a steel seat, with a proper holder, and a comfortable place to keep your legs. Invariably, it will be between Babu and his younger sister Manu, who used to grab that illusive seat. Since it was a free flowing seat, and his younger sister being just 6 years old, his father always gave Babu the benefit of doubt to take the "most wanted seat". Most wanted because the seat gave a panoramic view of all 3 sides for Babu to enjoy the ride to the maximum. His younger sister mostly ended up in front of his father next to steering, so that she was in control, and in the direct supervision of his father. That was all about the Lambretta drive from home to the Rhino movie Hall every Sunday.

Reaching the Rhino Hall, and the movie unfolding in front of you on the large 70mm screen itself was another great experience for Babu and his sister. Those days it was Amitabh Bachchan and his movies that were a craze among all school going kids, and Babu was no exception. Those days the movie must have run for a continuous 100 days in Rhino Hall, and Babu had seen it 5 times on a trot in the same screen. The movie Sholay had so much impact on Babu that for the initial two days he could not come to terms of Amitabh dying in the movie, and wanted a happy ending. He later realized that the director of the movie 'The Great Ramesh Sippy; had also shot another climax, and kept it ready, but people loved the tragic climax so much that the other ending never saw the light of day. Babu had also thought of a sequel to the cult classic Sholay, and even discussed the same with his sisters, and his friends. The movie craze was at its peak with Babu those days, and Rhino Hall had a big role to play.

Babu and his parents also used to go to Noonmati, maybe once every three months. Noonmati was a town, which was 25km away from Narangi, and the drive was a 45 minute ride. Babu loved every bit of the long drive. There was an uncle of Dad named Mr. Sundaresan who used to live in Noonmati, and used to invite Babu's dad and his family home for lunch once every 3 months. Post lunch, they will either go for a movie in Noonmati theatre, and one movie that comes to the mind of Babu was "Sharaabi", the classic movie of Amitabh Bacchhan with mesmerizing songs by Kishore Kumar.

Sometimes if Saturday is a Holiday for his father in office, then it will be a double treat for Babu and his family. The reason being apart from Noonmati, Babu and his sisters will be taken to Guwahati the capital city of Assam state. The distance time between Noonmati and Guwahati was 30 mins, and Babu will long for it, since the Guwahati trip will include a trip to Guwahati zoo, followed by a Chinese lunch at a restaurant in Guwahati city. The Guwahati zoo is always an awesome experience for Babu and his sisters, as they could see all animals in live captivity, performing their usual stunts in their respective cages. The best of the lot in the zoo was watching the gorillas and oranguttan's jumping and doing various stunts to the cheers of the audience watching, Babu being one of them. Another fun element in the zoo was the Otters floating, and running in the waters. It was absolute fun for Babu and his sisters whenever they visited the zoo with his Dad & Mom.

There was a scary part to the zoo as well, which Babu feared of, and that was the snake park enclosure. But since it was between the guerrillas and the crocodile shed, people could not avoid it, and had to make a visit to the enclosure as well. The one part that scared Babu to its wits was the python cage, where coiled pythons in twos' and fours' were coiled around the stem branch, and there used to be live chicken kept as feed for these pythons. The chickens were completely unaware that once the pythons get up from their sleep slumber, they will coil these chickens, and eat them in one gulp. That was the gory part of the zoo visit, but with repeated visits to the zoo, Babu managed to get the strength to withstand the fear of snake park. That was the lambretta drive with family to Noonmati and Guwahati on two-day holidays.

There was a scary experience once with the Lambretta scooter on a winter night, which Babu wants to be told to the readers as well. That night after watching a movie in Rhino Hall, the family had gone to a relative's house, and were returning home. It must be around 9.45pm, when the Lambretta scooter brake failed, and there was a slope down, followed by left or right turn to take Babu's father had only one option take right, which leads to the Guru Nanak temple on the left, and Kali Mandir on the right. Miracle so happened, that once the brake failed, and Babu' father had taken the right turn, the scooter did not stop, and after climbing 3 -4 steps of the Gurudwara, the lambretta scooter just stopped, and Babu and his family could alight safely without any injuries. There was a light scratch mark on the left hand of Babu's Father, and that's it. There seems to be a divine intervention from the Almighty and the family was saved from a major accident. Babu's father prayed to God, and asked Babu & his sisters to chant.. Jo Bole So Nihal..Satsriaakal. And they all chanted the same, and to this day whenever Babu passes through any Gurudwara, those prayer words will automatically come to his lips, and he will chant the words again. Thus, the Lambretta scooter ride had the fun and scary part entwined to it, and something that Babu always loved. The blue-white lambretta scooter was the pride of the house, and Babu enjoyed sitting at the back prima donna seat, and sometimes stood in front, when Dad asked him to be there.

One such journey which Babu remembers even to this day is the late night drive to officer's mess on the 23rd June, 1983, when the prudential World Cup Finals was going on in London at Lords. Kapil Dev and his Indian team had reached the finals, and were playing the mighty West Indies at Lords Cricket ground. Since London was 6 hrs behind of Indian time, hence the batting of India was over, and they had scored 183 runs. When Babu & his father reached Officer's mess, the time was around 9pm IST, and West Indies were batting. They were 4 down for 105 runs. It was Bacchus and Clive Lyod who were batting. Babu peeped into the television that was showing the match on a black & white television, and then a wicket fell, and west indies were 5 down, and still 76 runs to get. By then

Babu's father had finished the work, and took Babu back home. Babu was dreaming the whole night about what must have happened to the match. Next day morning, his father while going to the office told him, Babu Indian won the match and lifted the World Cup for the first time. The newspaper had Kapil Dev lifting the trophy, and a picture of the entire Indian cricket team. After his father had gone to office, Babu decided to cut the paper clip of Indian Team, since it also had Sunil Gavaskar, one of his school time idols, whose matches Babu used to listen to on the radio, and later on the Television too.

Chapter 7

RADIO: Murphy Radio

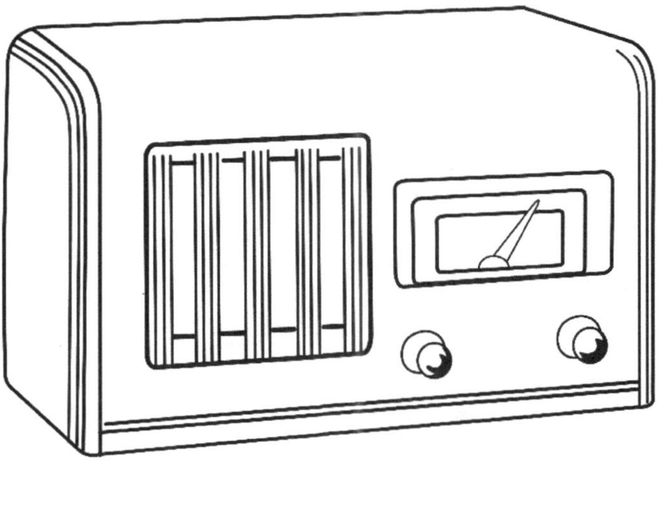

Babu was a cricket freak during the school times, so much so that Radio commentary was the flavour of the season then. One interesting incident which Babu still recalls was the Murphy small transistor radio he had, and which his father had given him to listen to songs and commentary as and when there was any cricket match of India.

In the year 1980 India was touring England, and playing a 5-Test series against Bob Willis. Babu still recalls listening to the Radio commentary with Bob Willis bowling, and it was Sunil Gavaskar and Sandeep Patil were at the crease. Gavaskar had completed his century, and Sandeep Patil was batting on 80 not out. There were 2 overs to go before lunch time, and Babu was glued to the radio. Babu had the habit of writing down the scores for his father and narrating the same to him, once he came back from tour.

That particular over is still vivid in the memory of Babu. In comes Willis, and bowls to Sandip Patil, and he has hit him for a four. He is 84 now. The next 5 balls something unimaginable was going to happen, and Babu would erupt in joy. The next 5 balls of Bob Wills were hit for four runs, and

Sandip Patil scored his century in double quick time. That feeling of joy was beyond control for Babu, and he wanted to tell his father immediately, so he wrote ball to ball commentary on a notebook for his father to read once he came back from tour. Such was his passion for cricket, and love for his father.

Also, to highlight at this stage is Television, since: Beltek TV was the first brand to arrive in their Narangi house in 1983, and Babu's father was the first person to own a television in the Narangi colony. Babu's family & the neighbourhood used the following programs

- Krishi Darshan@ 7pm, Chitrahar@8pm, The World This Week @10pm
- Buniyaad and, Yeh Jo Hai Zindagi serial @ 9pm and 9.30pm respectively

The advent of TV had taken Narangi by storm, and Babu was pleased to possess the first television in the locality, and used to call all his friends to watch the program together, and enjoy.

Chapter 8
Summer Holiday

The summer holidays of May-June month was something Babu & his sisters always used to look up to every year. Babu's parents were from the beautiful state of Kerala, and hence the summer vacations every year were to be spent in their mother's place. The best part of the summer holiday was the 5 day train journey, which Babu, his sisters, along with their parents had to undertake. The train journey had multiple stops, and only on the 5th morning, they reached Kerala from Guwahati. Let us now enjoy the train journey with Babu on one of his summer holidays. The first train they took was Kamrup Express from Guwahati to New Bongaigaon station.

It was an overnight 15 hr journey to reach New Bongaigaon from Guwahati. The best part of the journey was to see the long Brahmaputra river in its full glory from the train windows. During monsoon time on their return journey, which used to be at the end June, the monsoon will be at its peak, and to catch a glimpse of the gigantic Brahmaputra is a sight to behold.

From New Bongaigaon, there used to be another train that again takes 15 hour to reach Howrah Junction, which is the city name for Kolkata, the erstwhile Calcutta. One interesting stop, which Babu still remembers, is when the train reaches Malda junction at night, because then the train will cross the Farakka Garage, which is on the mighty Ganges river or Ganga. The bridge is so long that sometimes Babu will count, and the river seems to never end, so big was Ganga. Once in Howrah, the next train to Madras was only in the evening so Babu, his sisters and parents had half day time to move around Kolkata city. Hence, time to visit Victoria memorial, take a tram ride from Esplanade to Tollygunge, and have lunch in a Chinese restaurant, this used to be a typical half day routine for them as part of the halt at Kolkata. The next train they board is called Coromandel express, which takes a 30 hr time to reach Madras Central, known today as Chennai Central. Between Howrah and Madras, there used to be 3 to 4 major stops, which were Kharagpur, Waltair, Rajahmundry and Vijayawada. Each had its significance, and Babu's father used to tell him the same, which he so fondly remembers now.

Kharagpur has the longest platform, and is the largest station. Waltair is the name of the railway station, while the town is called Vizag or Vishakapatnam. Babu's chacha & chachi used to live in Vizag, and Babu fondly remembers even to this day, both will come with Idlis or dosas for Babu and his sisters to have during the train. Then comes Rajamundry station, because what comes after that is the gigantic river Godavari, so big that even today Babu tells his sister the river has two parts, the moment you thought the river was crossed on the bridge, there comes the 2nd leg of the river. Then comes Vijayawada around 3 in the evening. Babu and his sisters loved having vadas in the train, and evening tea used to be in Vijayawada with crispy vadas. Then comes the mighty Krishna river. One ritual that Babu so fondly remembers even to this day is throwing coins in the river, when the train crosses the river bridge. There was a fight for the window seat, and to throw the coin in such a manner that it goes straight into the river, without hitting the bridge. If AT ALL THE COIN HITS THE BRIDGE, THERE USED TO BE TRING SOUND, SO OTHERS COULD MAKE OUT, IT HIT THE STEEL BRIDGE.

Those days it was all about 5 paise, 10paise, and 25 paise coins, and Babu's mother used to carry the coins with her. She used to give one coin to Babu and to his sisters to pray to River God, and then throw the coin outside into the river water, without hitting the rail bridge. It was a challenge doing the same, and by the time Babu was in class 9, he had mastered the art of throwing coins exactly into the river, without hitting the steel bridge.

The train reaches Madras Central at 7pm, and there used to be a 3 hour gap, and the next train to Coimbatore will be late night at 11pm OR in case the train is booked the next morning, they have to spend the night in the sleeper class waiting room. Babu still remembers those days Madras was terribly hot, and the water used to taste salty both at the station and at any hotel in Madras Central. Babu always wished to reach Kerala fast to again enjoy fresh clean water. On the 5th day morning 6am, they take a train to Coimbatore, which reaches Kovai (nickname for Coimbatore) at 2.30pm. Babu & his parents have to quickly change the train, and jump into the train standing on another platform, which will take them to their final destination, which is Palghat junction (Today's Palakkad junction) in Kerala state.

Thus after a 5-day long journey on 5 different trains, they finally reach Kerala for their Summer Holidays. Babu will narrate his exciting summer holidays in the next edition of the book, so hold onto your excitement, and savor the Narangi Days, since there are two more chapters waiting to be read in this life-story of Babu.

Chapter 9

PET time Galore

One more interesting aspect of this story is the fondness and affection that Babu, and his sisters had for pet animals in Narangi. Babu's younger sister was crazy about pets, and will force her father to get one PET after another. They had all animal pets with them, one at a time, starting with a cat Julie, followed by a dog named Jimmy. They had a pair of rabbits for 6-months time, and loved feeding them carrots. But the rabbits created so much shit around that finally Babu's father had to return the same to the vendor.

Then came the arrival of two parrots, who were experts in mimicking the sound Babu and his sisters used to make. They became very much attached to Babu and his sisters. One Sunday morning, when Babu went outside the house, he could see lot of parrots around the cage making sound, maybe it was asking the two parrots of Babu to come out of the cage, and fly along with them. He then quickly called up his father and mother, and showed them the scene. By that time, Babu's sisters had also come outside the house, and we're watching the other parrots making noise, and saying something in their own language.

At that moment, Babu asked his father.. "Dad, can we release these two parrots from the cage? They will be so happy to return to their family, and will fly along on top of the skies." Babu's father said, "If your sisters are okay to part with the flowers, I am ready to release them." Babu now had to convince his sisters to accept the plan. It was a bit difficult, but Babu, as he is gifted with a nice way to handle any situation, did convince his sisters.

Now, it was evening, and time to say goodbye to the two parrots that Babu and his sisters had nurtured and taken care of for more than 6 months. His sisters were crying, but Babu in his heart of hearts was feeling lighter and happier that the parrots will be more happy with their family, and not in the cage. And, then his father opened the cage, and within 5 seconds, both the parrots flew out, and sat on a tree next to their house, and started making some noise. Babu's father told him and his sisters probably they were thanking us for letting them fly out into the open skies. Within 10 minutes, we could see a few parrots came, and our two parrots flew happily into the skies. It was a really happy moment for Babu and his family at Narangi.

Chapter 10

Vishwakarma Puja Festival

It was total celebration time for Babu, his family, and his friends starting with Vishwakarma Puja on September 17, followed by Durga Puja- Kali Puja a month later for one full week, culminating with Diwali with crackers, and lighting of Diyas.

Babu's father was in Defence, and hence all defence colonies used to celebrate September 17 in a grand way as Vishwakarma Puja. There used to be a stage function organized on the occasion, and Babu's father used to be the main organizer of the function. There used to be skits, drama, patriotic songs, and dance, followed by a grand dinner for all residents.

Babu and his sisters used to take part actively in these program, and the practice used to start 10 days before the program. You name the patriotic song, and Babu and his friends would have sung that song in Vishwakarma Puja. Boys and girls had separate line in the patriotic song, and each one used to sing more loudly on the mike to outwit the other. Babu's father was a great actor too, and in one of the Puja celebration recreated a scene from the epic Ramayana, with himself playing Lord Rama. The best part being Varghese uncle with his long moustache was Ravana the demon. The funny part, which Babu want to highlight here is the role being enacted by Caimal uncle who was Meghnath. In one of the scenes, when he is scolding Vibhishan, he stamps on the stage so hard that the stage wood gave away, and both him and Ravana went down the stage. The crowd went berserk on seeing this, but luckily nothing happened since foam was kept below the stage, as a result both Caimal uncle and Varghese uncle fell on it, and rose back into the stage like a phoenix.

This was one funny moment that Babu still recalls even today, and each Vishwakarma Puja day of September 17, it rekindles the memory.

Festivities continue with Durga Puja, during which time Babu and his sisters will get new dresses to wear and they will visit all Durga Puja pandals, and on the Mahanavami day, there used to be a Bhog Khichdi in Narangi Kali Mandir, which Babu, his sisters and parents used to visit every year. There will be many food stalls, and always Varghese uncle's dosa, which will serve crispy plain and masala dosa to all people visiting his stall.

The full year of fun, studies, play, and masti, though ends for Babu in December month by visiting the Church along with his best friend Shaji. They used to visit the church for midnight carols, and later the next day Shajis's parents would send cakes home for Babu and his sisters.

All in all, Narangi days were all about love, brotherhood, fun, study all encompassed into the lives of Babu, which has only been narrated in parts.

The next edition of the book will focus on the summer holidays of Babu... so hold on till such time the next edition is out.

About the Author

Manoj Kumar Nair...MK for friends and family is a corporate marketing professional with 3 decades of experience in the healthcare industry, having worked in many large Indian and Multinational healthcare companies based in Mumbai, Delhi, Bangalore and Chennai city respectively. MK is a product of Kendriya Vidyalaya and did his schooling from KVs across the country, since his father was connected to Defence Services. Exposure to various states honed his personality skills. MK was a master quizzer who won many Quiz contests in schools and colleges, including participation in the once famous "Sports Quiz" program anchored by Dr. Narottam Puri for Doordarshan in early 1990s, and winning a prize in the Delhi finals. MK did his graduation degree from Manipal, and a postgraduate program in business administration from Mumbai University. MK is happily married to Jayasree, and he has two sons Sharath and Shyam. MKs passion include watching sports, and singing in corporate events and family get togetherS. He is an avid movie buff, and Amitabh Bacchhan and Shahrukh Khan are his favourite actors. His sports idols include Sunil Gavaskar, Sachin Tendulkar, MS Dhoni, Roger Federer and Lionel Messi. Some of his best favourite authors include Robin Sharma, Shiv Khera, and Simon Sinek. There was always a passionate writer within him, and the inspiration started bearing fruits after the masterclass live sessions with author and mentor Geetika Saigal in the year 2022. MK then enrolled in her 3-month course on book writing, and understood the skills to be honed to become a successful author. And, the result is this book titled "The Narangi Days", to be published in 2024. MK consider this first book as the greatest gift from Almighty God, which is hitting the stands, both online and offline for the people to read and enjoy from Beeja publishing house. Grab a copy soon, and happy reading for my book readers, and to all my well-wishers too.

Do write back to me with your love and feedback on *nair.kumarmanoj@gmail.com*